Stock Market Investing For Beginners - The Investment Guide - How to benefit from the crisis, invest in stocks and generate long-term passive income incl. ETF and Stock Picking Checklist

William K. Bradford

Copyright © [2020] [William K. Bradford]

All rights reserved

The author of this book owns the exclusive right to its content. Any commercial usage or reproduction requires the clear consent of the author.

ISBN – 9798656141345

Table of Contents

Chapter 1 – Introduction 1

Chapter 2 - Developing the Mindset of an Investor 7

Thinking on the Razor's Edge 9

Standing Up Against Fear 10

Saying No to Greed 11

Create Guidelines. Stick to Your Rules. 12

Chapter 3 - Getting Your Life Ready to Invest 15

Preparing Your Financial Situation 15

Consider Your Retirement 18

Chapter 4 - What Kind of Investor Are You? **20**

Pre-Investor 20

Passive Investor 21

Active Investor 23

Chapter 5 - Opening your First Investor Accounts **27**

Introducing the Brokerage Account 28

Chapter 6 - Your First Look into Learning About Stocks **32**

Creating Your Dream Portfolio 34

Education and Knowledge on Your Industry 35

Making the Key Decision 36

Stock Choosing Metrics to Consider 37

Chapter 7 - How to Choose the Right Stocks for You 41

Researching Stocks and Using

Fundamental Stock Analysis 43

Introducing Qualitative Data.. 43

Introducing Quantitative Data... 45

Using the Data to Make Decisions 47

How to Avoid Illegitimate Sources of

Stock Information 48

Look for Legitimate Sources... 48

Consider Context and 'Cherry Picking' 49

How Legit is Your Writer?.. 50

Look at the Writer's History.. 50

Avoid Penny Stock News.. 51

Dismiss Bot Content.. 52

Use Common Sense 52

Chapter 8 - The Complete Stock Picking Checklist...55

Chapter 9 - Setting an Investment Budget..60

How to Set an Investment Budget................................ 61

Chapter 10 - Choosing Your Long-Term Investment Strategies 65

Strategy #1 – Growth Investment................................ 66

Strategy #2 – Value Investment.................................... 69

Strategy #3 – Dollar-Cost Investment.......................... 72

Strategy #4 – Momentum Investment 74

A Mention of Short Selling... 77

Chapter 11 - How to Benefit from Investing in a Crisis.................**79**

How to Take Advantage of a Financial Crisis......................... 80

Focus on Low-Risk Investments.................................. 83

Look for Consumer Staple Investments.................................. 84

Look for Recession-Proof Opportunities 84

Diversify Your Portfolio...................................... 85

Consider Dividend Stocks................................ 85

Consider Precious Metal Investments......................... 86

Chapter 12 - What is an EFT, and Why Is It Important?.................**88**

What is an ETF, and How Does It Work?................................ 89

The Benefits of Buying ETFs... 91

Cheaper, More Affordable Costs 92

The Tax Benefits of ETFs... 94

How to Buy and Sell ETFs.. 95

Chapter 13 - Moving Forward with

Your Portfolio (Final Thoughts) 96

Disclaimer...98

Chapter 1 – Introduction

When you hear the word' investor,' what do you see?

Maybe you get the vision of some crazy, loud-mouthed, pinstripe-suited guy shouting and screaming at another pinstripe-suited guy, waving around bits of paper around and getting incredibly sweaty at screens displaying with numbers and graphs. The room is thick and hot with testosterone and passion. Come five o'clock, a bell rings, the floor falls silent, and everyone goes home to rest before it all kicks off again the next day.

In the past, and definitely in some places today, that specific image isn't too far from the truth, but it's not the entire truth. At our very cores, we are all investors. I am. You are. Your neighbours and family are. You go to school or take online courses because you want to invest in yourself and your future. You save money in your savings account so you can go on vacation next year. You create a college fund for your children because you want to invest in their future.

What does it mean to invest? It means taking action today because you believe in the value it's going to have tomorrow. Or next week. Or a few years from now. Investing is something we all do at some point in our lives in one form or another, but if you're reading this book, then know you've taken a step to take your investment instincts one step further.

We're talking about the world stock market investment.

While lots of people in today's world aim to save for their future, investors seek to create more money to see them through their lives comfortably and beyond. It's not about how much money you can save; it's about how much money you can make.

If you've envisioned of buying that dream house, the dream car, going on that dream around-the-world adventure, or you've just wanted to wake up in the morning knowing you've got enough money in the bank that you don't even need to stress about your finances, now is the time to start working towards that. Imagine that. No money concerns. Just getting up and getting on with your day because you know everything is taken care of financially. While a pipedream for many, investors take steps to turn that fantasy into a reality.

There's no denying there's a lot of money to be made investing in stocks. You've probably heard of the likes of Jordan Belfort, the Wall Street investor who made millions on the stock market, made famous by the movie The Wolf of Wall Street. While an extreme and dramatized case, real-life investment heroes like Warren Buffett are considered by many to be the most successful stock investor of all-time. Buffett even provides financial advice to presidents and political leaders in countries around the world. Just a word from someone like Buffett can shift market forces around the world in a heartbeat.

Again, these are extreme and mainstream cases. There are hundreds of thousands of investors around the world. Some make millions, while others make a few thousand dollars a year on top of their salary. The investment industry is one of those industries where you get out as much as you put in. There are no limits to how far you can go; it's just a case of whether you're willing to go there.

But, okay, let's slow down a minute. If you're coming into the world of investing in the stock market for the first time, it can be a big, scary, and overwhelming place. There's seemingly lots to learn, lots of jargon to wrap your head around, and then there are all the horror stories of people who may have lost so much making the wrong decisions.

This is why this book is in your hands. This is your first step into understanding everything you need to know about the practice of investing in stocks and making it a profitable pastime, whether you're doing investing as a side hustle or plan to make it a full-time venture. Take a moment to think about what this could bring into your life.

Financial security. The freedom to do what you want and go where you please. Less stress. Less financial anxiety. More money to look after your family and your children. The security of knowing that even if something goes wrong in your life, you have the money in place to ensure it doesn't become a problem.

By taking the time to invest in yourself and learning what you need to know when it comes to investing, you'll maximise your chances of getting it right. You'll create and build up your portfolio, start investing in stocks, and ultimately start making money.

Don't worry, the stock market may seem like a very daunting place, and everything can change in a single day or even a single hour. The fast-paced nature of it all is enough to put anybody off.

Everything you need to help guide you through the step up and educate you is right here in this book.

Throughout the following chapters, we're going to explore everything you need to know to become a full-fledged stock investor. We'll cover what mindset you need and how to get you and your life ready to introduce the very idea of investing in stocks. Once you're ready, you'll define what kind of investor you want to be and what direction you want to take.

You'll then learn about opening your first trading account and learn everything you need to know about choosing the right stocks that are right for you. You'll read all about setting a budget, creating a portfolio and investment strategy, and ultimately cover everything essential when it comes to maximising your profit and minimising your losses.

We'll even talk about how to make money during a global economic crisis, and some of the more recent opportunities that have been added to the stock trading world. Anyway, that's enough from me, let's get the ball rolling.

Chapter 2 - Developing the Mindset of an Investor

Becoming an investor in the stock market is not for the faint-hearted. Before you even think about buying your first stock, you need to get your mind in the right place.

In many respects, stock investment is a lot like gambling; at least that's how many people see it. The risks are high, and the rewards are thrilling. The losses can indeed be devastating, but these are only extreme cases, yet you should never forget that it could happen to you. One wrong decision made from a place of stress can cost you everything.

I don't say this to scare you or freak you out, but I say it to open your eyes to the indisputable fact that it's essential you keep your mind clear and your emotions out of the way when venturing into the stock market world. Developing your mindset into the mindset of an investor is perhaps the most crucial part of this process. If your mind isn't right, you're going to make mistakes, and it's going to cost you.

How your mind works is at the core of being a successful investor and will be what makes or breaks you. There are going to be times during your investment career when things get tough. You may make a mistake or an unforeseen event that plummets your stock down to nothing.

This can leave you feeling shallow and empty, as though everything has gone wrong and you've lost everything. The opposite is also true. You'll experience exhilarating highs where you're making so much return on your capital, and you just ride that wave, thinking it's never going to end.

It's at this exact moment when emotions like this come into play that you're going to make an unthoughtful, emotion-fuelled decision that costs you everything or pulls you back from the brink. Having a mind that can notice and overcome these emotions, enabling you to stay focused is not something you're born with, but rather a mindset you need to train yourself to have. Here are some of the traits you'll need to develop.

Thinking on the Razor's Edge

There's no doubt that one of the best mindset traits an investor needs is being able to make snap decisions at the drop of a hat. For many people, when the pressure is on (especially when that pressure arises from seemingly nowhere), everything can seem too much. With a mind clouded by stress and overwhelm, you're not going to be making the best, most informed, nor most educated decisions you can.

A stock market investor needs to be present in the moment, focused, and disciplined. Stocks come in one minute and out the next, and during this rapid time frame, you must be able to keep your emotions out and your mind in gear.

Being a stock investor means you have the discipline to stick to your trading plan and don't let profits or losses get to your head. You'll understand this a lot more as we go on, but for now, just focus on developing discipline.

Standing Up Against Fear

When you've just invested a ton of money into one stock, and then you hear the terrible news nobody wants to hear, it's easy to lose yourself to fear. The stock is plummeting. The market has crashed. It's easy to feel afraid and that everything you've worked so hard to build is about to fall apart. It's natural for any sane human being to feel this way.

Being able to face these fears and stay focused and on plan, being able to notice the feeling of fear and overcome it, is what separates the good investors from the bad. It's practically effortless to overreact to bad news or focus on one mistake in your past that can unconsciously hold you back from taking necessary, profitable risks both now and in the future.

The best way to deal with this crippling fear is to bring awareness to it. If you don't know you're scared and are basically just running with the fear and making decisions through it, you're going to fall.

Instead, take a breath and think, "Okay, I'm fearful. This is natural. Now, what am I going to do about it?" This kind of mindset and way of thinking grounds you and helps you stay in the game. You need to be proactive in training your brain to work in this way, although much of it will come with experience.

Saying No to Greed

When you're high on an investment win streak, you feel like it's never going to end, and it's easy to keep going until you fall, leaving yourself broken-hearted and without anything to show for what you've already done.

Of course, we're talking about getting greedy with your investments, something that will only ever lead to your downfall.

The greedy always get caught out, and there's a saying on Wall Street claiming that '(the) pigs get slaughtered.' Being able to overcome a greedy mindset will come with experience and practice but being conscious that greed is a real mental obstacle you'll need to overcome will go a long way.

Start focusing on this trait now. Start developing your discipline because you're going to need it long-term, especially if you become successful with your trades.

Create Guidelines. Stick to Your Rules.

We'll talk about this point a little more in-depth later on, but the key to becoming a successful investment stock trader is developing and creating a financial plan, and then sticking to it. It takes discipline and willpower to stick to your plan, especially when you feel completely demotivated when something has gone wrong, or you're riding high on the waves of success.

No matter what situation you find yourself in, you need to remember and stick with your investment strategy. It's there for a reason. Don't give up on it so quickly. The trick to investment is being able to take both wins and losses as equals.

As with all these mindset guidelines, you need to know how to ground yourself when the going gets tough. If you're the sort of person who is currently very reactive in your life and easily triggered by events, you should consider whether stock trading is for you. A successful investor can take emotion, both positive and negative, out of the equation. Stick to your plan. Don't deviate off course on a complete whim or just because something isn't going your way.

When you start developing these mindset traits, you'll start developing a true investor's mindset. This mindset will help you succeed and ensures you have set up your values to help you make decisions. When you find yourself in an intense and emotionally driven situation, you'll have already developed the tactics needed to ground yourself and then move forward, minimising the risk of making the wrong decisions.

All these mindset traits may seem fairly obvious, but it's hard to remember them when you're in the heat of the moment. Throughout the following chapters, we'll refer back to these points in context, but you must have them in mind before continuing into the stock market world. If not, you could be jeopardising yourself drastically.

Chapter 3 - Getting Your Life Ready to Invest

Okay, so you've got your mindset in check, and you're ready to start investing. It's a big step to make your first investment, so you'll want to make sure you really are ready. By this, I mean making sure your life is ready. Let's talk about some things you're going to want to think about before making your initial stock purchase.

Preparing Your Financial Situation

First things first. Make sure you've already paid off any debt you owe. If you're trading stocks while you're in debt, or your debts aren't under control, there's a very high chance you're going to put yourself into a bad financial position.

This is because the interest you have to pay on your debts will typically outweigh the return you have on your original investments. If you're getting a return of 4% on your investments, but you're paying 19% interest on your credit card, you're not making any money.

When you start building up your portfolio and buying and selling more because you've established your footing in the industry, this is where you'll make big money. On the other hand, when you're starting out, the returns are small. If you have money in stocks and debt to pay off, things can get tight, and you may struggle to pay the bills. You can't spread yourself too thinly.

Next, make sure you have some kind of savings. Just as we spoke about above, you need to make sure you're preparing yourself in case you experience a rainy day. This means if something does go wrong in your life and you're strapped for cash and unable to live, you've got a small sum to fall back on—an emergency fund for when you have no other options.

Of course, you'll be hoping you'll never need to access this fund, and all will go well, but you never what curveball life is going to throw your way. As a stock investor, the more prepared you are, the less of a problem you'll need to deal with. Imagine if you're tightly living while trying to make money on stocks, and your car is totalled, and you need several thousand dollars to get a new one. If you have no savings and all your money is tied up in stocks, this isn't a position you want to be in.

As a general rule of thumb, most experienced investors will say to save at least three months of your salary. Put it into a separate bank account before you invest anything at all. Try and find an account with a high interest rate, so you can make some money while storing it, and never, ever access this money to use it for investment purposes.

Thirdly, since a stock investor's financial journey is up and down all the time, and you're guaranteed to have good days and bad days, it's always worth thinking about getting yourself some insurance. You never know if you're going to find yourself in an accident, or you may get sick and find you're unable to work nor invest.

If you can't work, you can't make money, and if you have a family or people to look after, this can be bad news for them. This is why it pays to get yourself an insurance policy like critical illness cover and life insurance. Again, this is something you hope you're never going to need, but it's always best to be prepared.

Consider Your Retirement

Your retirement might be a long way off, or it may be just around the corner. Either way, your state pension will probably not allow you to live a comfortable lifestyle for the rest of your life. If you want a nice life during your elderly years, you're going to need to think about preparing for them.

So much preparation, right?

If you want to be comfortable, you're going to want to think about saving around $20,000 a year. This figure is an average that most people will be able to live off comfortably. $27,000 is you're a couple. If you want luxury holidays every year and some adventures here and there, you're probably looking more around the $33,000 to $42,000 mark.

This means for a standard 20-year retirement; you're going to need to save around $232,200, or $481,000 for the luxury retirement. With standard pension rates around $8,700 a year, you're going to need to get saving.

Plan these saving goals into your investment plan. You need to think about what kind of retirement you want, set goals on how much you need to keep, and then start saving it. You need to be thinking about this before you start investing because it needs to be in your strategy.

Some other investment opportunities you may wish to think about here include;

- Contributing to a workplace pension

- Contributing to your private pension

- Saving from your job income packet

- Saving from your investment profits

- Looking into tax breaks and retirement schemes

Now that you've considered these key aspects of your life, you're one step closer to becoming an investor.

Chapter 4 - What Kind of Investor Are You?

What kind of investor you are will determine everything. How much you're investing, what stocks you're buying, and what level of control over you have over your portfolio, so you'll want to decide what type you're interested in. There are three main types to choose from.

Pre-Investor

Unless you're fortunate and born into wealth, everyone starts as a pre-investor, which basically refers to someone who is not an investor in any way. There are no investments made, no stocks purchased, and you'll probably have minimal financial consciousness.

This type of investor probably has no retirement plan or pension and only has one because their workplace set it up on their behalf. You may live paycheck to paycheck and haven't really taken up the responsibility of your finances. If you haven't invested before, then you're a pre-investor.

For the purposes of this book, and the fact you're reading it, I'm going to assume that you want to move out of this category.

Passive Investor

Not everyone wants control over a portfolio and simply aren't interested in the thrills of monitoring the stock markets and trading stocks. If you're going to invest to make money, but you have no real interest in managing a portfolio or learning the ropes needed to become an investor, this is known as being a passive investor.

Some people say that around 90% of investors will fall into this category. Within this investor group type, you'll have some assets under your name, and you may contribute to your workplace's pension. You may also be involved in some investment schemes, such as premium bonds, ISA savings accounts, or even cryptocurrency investment.

Sometimes, your bank may give you shares in a company or their finances through dividends, which can be sold at any time. However, while you may have investments here and there, you don't really know what's going on, and you're relying on the experience of another person and their investment strategy to help you make you a bit of money.

In most cases, you'll need to pay some kind of commission to the person or investment service that's managing your portfolio, but you'll need to think about what your service is doing and how they're treating your finances.

For example, some banks will buy and sell stocks using the money in your bank account and aim to make money. They will then take a commission, pay you a sum, and then invest the rest of the profits to make more money. While this can work at making a bit of money, many services like this will invest on safe stocks to guarantee a return as much as they can, meaning you're probably not going to see any significant changes in your bank balance figure.,

It's entirely possible to create enough wealth to live on in this way if you're using it in addition to your salary, but it just takes a lifetime of little gains. If you're working a full-time job and investing on the side, this is perfect because you'll get a little extra profit in your bank account and you don't have to overthink it at all.

However, if you're looking to trade stocks full-time or you want to make a large amount of wealth to live off, you'll want to be thinking about the final investor archetype, the active investor.

Active Investor

The active investor. Individuals ready to give their all buying and selling stocks, treating the venture as a full-time business. When you plan on becoming an active investor, you can be sure you're about to get very intimate with the stock market.

What mainly separates an active investor from the other types of investor is the fact that you not only receive profits back from passive investments, for example, through investing in stocks, selling them, and making a profit, but you get the experience of how the industry works and how it's run.

With this experience, you'll be able to make experience-based decisions that pay off over the long-term, because you'll have the skills that no other investor type. This means you get a return from your trades and long-term profit from your investment into your skills as an investor.

In short, the more you trade, the more experience you get, and therefore the better trader you become. Your potential becomes limitless.

More importantly, an active investor can trade any time, in whatever way they like. It doesn't matter what the market conditions are; you'll be able to invest how you want and be proactive in minimising your losses as much as possible and then reinvesting to make money as the market's flux in the other direction. It's all on you and how you want to do things

Of course, learning when to buy and when to sell, choosing which stocks you want to invest in, and learning how to read the markets takes time and energy. You're not going to get it right every time, but you do have full control over the direction you want to make.

This is vital. Active investors understand at their very cores that small investments and small profits in the short-term can build up and create massive, sustainable earnings over the long-term, and that's how real wealth is generated and returned. It's all about maximising your return on capital.

Active investors also understand that it's not about trying to earn as much as possible; it's about maximising how much money your money can make, and how long you can compound your profits. This means minimises losses as much as you can, on top of maximising profits.

For the rest of this book, we're going to be focusing on what it means to get started as an active investor. When you're starting out, you don't need to quit your day job or sell everything to maximise your starting capital. You just need to keep your head on your shoulders and start building experience and your own portfolio.

If you're looking to jump in and really go for being an investor, eventually planning to make it your full-time job, that works. Your beginning and introduction to the stock market trading will start the same. How far you're willing to take yourself is entirely up to you.

Just to quickly summarise;

Pre-Investor	Someone who doesn't invest in any, has no interest in investing, and usually not secure financially
Passive Investor	Someone who is in control of their money and invests but doesn't pay much attention. Pays into their workplace pensions and probably has ISA savings
Active Investor	Someone who is incredibly proactive in their investments. Will read up on companies, have a trading account, and will invest in stocks and bonds.

Chapter 5 - Opening your First Investor Accounts

We've already covered getting started with your mindset and defined what kind of investor you're going to be. I know it's a lot of preparation and getting things set up, but you want to make sure you're walking into this world with your best foot first. Good news though, we're finally ready to start the real investment process.

It begins with opening your investment accounts.

In the following chapter, we're going talk about opening your first investment account, detailing what one is and how it works, and how you can use it to manage and grow your portfolio. Let's begin.

Introducing the Brokerage Account

The primary type of account you're going to be working with is your brokerage account. This is a financial account like any other, but it will set up through an investment brokerage firm. Unlike your traditional bank accounts, such as your credit card or current account, you'll have the ability to purchase and hold all kinds of investment opportunities, including;

- Stocks

- Mutual funds

- Bonds

- ETFs

Sometimes, these accounts are also known as 'taxable accounts,' since any income you make on your investments within this account is taxable as under capital gains. All brokerage accounts are offered and upheld by a brokerage firm, of which there are many to choose from.

Some full-on services will be quite pricey to set up and may require a large of money to start you off. For example, Cobra Trading requires a $30,000 minimum deposit to get you started. On the other hand, some accounts require nothing, and you can set them up for free.

Nowadays, you should be able to open any of the brokerage accounts you can find and want to work with online, and it should only take a matter of minutes. No matter what account you choose to work with, you'll need to deposit an investment of some degree so that you can buy stocks.

Remember, all the money and the investments made through and kept in your brokerage account will always belong to you. The brokerage firm is simply the middleman that hosts the account. You can have as many or as few brokerage accounts as you want, and there are no limits on how much money you can deposit.

So, how do you choose a brokerage account?

There are two main account types to choose from; Robo-advisor accounts and online brokers. If you're looking for control over your own account and you just want to be left to your own devices, you'll want an online brokerage account.

With your own account, you can buy and sell all the investment types we spoke about above, and you'll have complete freedom to what you want when you want.

On the other hand, a Robo-advisor account, also known as a 'managed brokerage account,' takes away your control and instead uses advanced computer algorithms to predict, choose, and manage what investments your account deals with. All you need to do is simply choose your financial goals and what kind of timeline you want to be working to.

If you want to be an active investor, but also semi-passive, like if you have a day job for example, and don't have all the time in the world to invest into the world of stock trading, this could be a good option, at least until you're able to find your feet and make enough money that you can start investing more time into it.

There are plenty of comparison websites online where you can easily compare both kinds of brokerage accounts, their fees and prices, and what kind of features they're offering, all of which can be found with a quick online search. Alternatively, you can manually search and look through individual brokerage websites to see what accounts are on offer. Still, it's really up to you and what kind of investment you're going to be working with.

Typically, you'll need to be over 18 years old to create an account. However, parents can open accounts on their children's behalf, and the process is merely heading over to your chosen brokerage account website, and then signing up by making your way through the sign-up form.

When you're happy with your account and are ready to go, simply deposit, however much money you want to start spending (don't worry, we talk more about setting this amount later). Once it's in your account (usually instantly), it's time to buy stocks.

Chapter 6 - Your First Look into Learning About Stocks

Damn, didn't your heart just skip a beat then? You're ready to buy your first stocks. If you're following this book as your guide, you're probably sitting on your brokerage account's homepage or stock page, looking at all those lovely stocks backed by all those reds, greens, and confusing numbers.

Don't worry; it's this confusing to everyone, to begin with. You'll get there in time and looking at these charts of data will become second nature to you—no need to feel overwhelmed. Let's just take things one step at a time.

With tens of thousands of stocks to choose from, you may be left scratching your head. Which ones are worth buying? How do you know you're picking a good stock or a stock that's about to crash? How do you know which stock is better between two or three various stocks?

Slow down. There are three main things you want to think about first.

- Your portfolio goals and direction you want to go

- Your education and experience with certain industries

- Combining the two principles to buy and sell stocks

Unfortunately, there's no hard and fast way to choose, buy, and sell stocks. Every stock is a risk because you can never guarantee what's going to happen in the real world. But that doesn't mean you can't accurately predict what's happening based on the knowledge you're educating yourself with.

Let's break it down.

Creating Your Dream Portfolio

Firstly, you're going to want to decide what kind of portfolio you want. Do you want to be trading on the tech industry's frontline, or is sustainable energy a personal passion of yours? There are endless industries out there you can invest in on the stock market; it's just about taking the time to choose one that suits you.

The trick is to choose an industry or niche you want to work with, but then you need to make sure you're sticking with it. If you stick with an industry for a few months and get bored and switch over to another industry and basically start again, this is nowhere near the amount of time that it takes to make it big on the stock market.

Once you've decided what industry you're going with, you're going to want to stick with it for a few months, or even years, to come. This is where you'll see the best payoffs and returns.

Of course, some industries are riskier than others. If you're investing in the latest Silicon Valley apps and end up flopping, you'll lose money. If you invest in retail companies that remain the same or steadily grow over time, then your money is considered much safer. But, with higher risk tends to come higher rewards.

That's the critical decision you'll need to make.

Education and Knowledge on Your Industry

Now comes the active part of being an active investor. You need to start educating yourself on the markets to see what's happening and what's trending. Knowledge is indeed power. You need to read news articles and watch experts talk about what's going on and make your own decision based on their shared information.

Hopefully you've chosen an industry you're passionate about, which is more exciting and educational than boring and monotonous. Let's say you're investing in tech giants, and Facebook is rumoured to have a new feature coming out in several months.

Facebook stocks are cheap right now, so you buy them, wait a couple of months, and there you go. The feature was successful, and you've made money. You can now sell the stocks and make money. However, two months on from this, Facebook then buys another virtual reality company, and the stocks skyrocket further, meaning if you had held out, you would have made more money.

If you had known that Facebook was going to buy the virtual reality company, you would have the information that could have made you more, helping you understand the best times to sell.

This brings us onto the final point.

Making the Key Decision

By feeding yourself and consuming information about companies within your industry, observing industry trends, and staying up to date with daily news, you'll be able to decide which stocks you want to buy and when.

Stock trading is all about keeping your eyes open for a new opportunity. You may open the newspaper one day or read an article on a blog somewhere that could turn into the core foundation of an investment decision. This is all it takes to have what you need to buy stocks.

If you want to play it safe, you may want to use 'common sense' observations. If a company says they're going to launch a new product to an emerging market, then yes, it's probably a good idea to invest in that company because they'll be making a lot more money soon and you'll get your return on your capital.

On the other hand, you may want to take risks. Say Facebook has another scandal, and it destroys its stock value. You could buy now when the market is low if you believe Facebook is going to recover, and you'll get your investment back and more. Again, this is where you need to balance the pros and cons of a decision and make it yourself.

Stock Choosing Metrics to Consider

There are some other factors you'll want to be aware of when making a stock purchasing decision. For example, how reliable is the source of information you're choosing to listen too? Is it an authority news website or blog, or is it some hidden blog you just happened to stumble across?

You need to make sure you're critical of your sources and using due diligence. Once you're happy that the information you're using is legitimate, only then should you be making the decision to buy or sell. We'll talk about this in way more detail in a following chapter, but I know you're eager to get on with buying.

Another tip to remember is looking at choosing a handful of companies to work around. Of course, this is the very nature of selecting stocks. You need to find companies that you think are going to make money and then invest in them to get a return in the future. There are numerous ways you can do this.

If you have some companies in mind that you'd like to invest in already, that's great. If not,

By conducting an online search, which is as easy as typing' tech industry ETFs', for example, you'll be able to see the top stocks and the trading information for each. Many ETFs will also enable you to break down your search criteria by factors like;

| Market Cap | Market cap is the total cost of all the stocks a company has. For example, if a company has |

	100 stocks at $1,000, the market cap would be $100,000.
P/E Ratio	This metric takes a company's market capitalization and then divides this number by their annual earnings. This then calculates how affordable or expensive a stock is, and how much you should be willing to pay. A great metric for comparing companies within the same industry.
PEG Ratio	Stands for 'price-to-earnings' ratio. You take the P/E ratio and divide it by the expected earnings growth rate. Again, this metric is used to track prices of stocks and compare with comparable businesses.

Debt-to-Equity	If a company has a lot of debt, especially when compared to their equity, this can indicate a business is going through tough economic times, and you may want to avoid buying stock with them.
Dividend Yield	Simply put, if a company stock is worth $100 per share, and the dividend payout is $5, this the dividend yield is 5%.
Payout Ratio	If you want to see how often dividends are paid out of a company, a clear indicator that it's profitable, this is the metric you want to be looking at.

Don't follow if you're just starting and you don't know what these means, just focusing on mastering the basics and build these into your vocabulary as you gain more experience.

Again, it's all about getting as much information as you can before choosing which companies and stocks to invest in. You'll develop your own style and way of selecting companies and stocks as you go and get better at trading, but considering everything we've spoken about should be a decent starting point.

Chapter 7 - How to Choose the Right Stocks for You

Continuing from the last chapter, whether you win or lose trading on the stock market will depend on one core factor above all else; the stocks you choose to buy and sell. Making this choice is hard. You could spend hours, if not days, staring at computer screens and financial sections in your preferred newspaper, trying to figure out what will work and what won't.

If you want to make any money, sooner or later, you're going to have to make a decision, but thankfully I've compiled this guide that can help. We already spoke about this in the last chapter, but there's so much we can deep dive into in the topic of using information to pick your stocks, this entire chapter will be dedicated to it. From here, we've going to cover the following topics;

- Researching stocks and understanding the business

- How to use quantitative and qualitative analysis data

- How to avoid emotion in your decision-1 process

- How to diversify your portfolio to spread risk

There are many approaches and strategies you can use, many of which we'll speak about later on in another chapter. Still, for now you're going to want to focus on the mindset and skills you need to have when choosing stocks, using the information and data processing methods above.

These methods are interchangeable, if not essential, with whatever investment strategy you choose to use, so don't get hung up and thinking you can't use one for your strategy. Each strategy can be adapted to suit your own needs and goals; you just need to understand the basics to get started.

Researching Stocks and Using Fundamental Stock Analysis

Fundamental stock analysis is the process you'll undergo when deciding whether you buy a stock or not. It's the crème da le crème of information processing that you'll use to back your decision. This fundamental data can be broken down into two separate segments: qualitative and quantitative. Let's break down both.

Introducing Qualitative Data

This one is simple.

The first type of data is real-world data that refers to the company's goings-on on the stock market. You may be looking at press releases from the company, news on the company website, blog, or social media pages. Good news means people will buy stocks, and bad news means people will sell their stock. If a company is not looking good, and nobody is buying anything, the stock will go down, and people will sell.

However, this could be the ideal time to buy if the sales department manager has just been fired, and they hire some top shot from another company, meaning the stocks could be aligned to rise dramatically, but more on that later.

You can look into staffing structures, financial events the company goes through, whether that's rebranding or holding a sale, and other similar situations all companies go through. You may follow the company on LinkedIn and notice they hire a new manager for a department. The reputation of a business plays a considerable part in its stock market value, and you need to be considering what's going on within a company.

Other significant events, like political upset, an event like Brexit, or the COVID-19 pandemic, can also cause a massive fluctuation in the stock market. Make sure you're considering large-scale events that happen on a country-wide scale, or even internationally or globally. Consider that Tesla CEO Elon Musk smoked marijuana on the Joe Rogan podcast causing Tesla stock to drop 11% instantly.

This is what I mean by qualitative data. There's a bountiful amount of data out there that can be used, as long as you're checking to make sure it's coming from a legitimate source. All of this can be used to determine whether a stock will go up or down, thus aiding your purchasing decisions.

Introducing Quantitative Data

On the other hand, we have quantitative data. This kind of data refers to the hard-financial data of a company and ignores the company's inner workings or the courts of public opinion. Instead, it looks at the real figures of what a company is making and what they are doing. Since each company of the stock market is a public company, finding this information is not as difficult as it may sound.

This means you could be looking at stats like earning release sheets, an essential document that many investors keep a keen eye on. On the earnings sheets, you'll see clearly whether a company is making or losing money. It's all well and good pricing a stock at a certain value, but if the company's financial data doesn't reflect this value, you know you need to think about what it's true value is and whether this is a stock you can make money from.

From here, you'll want to start looking at documents like a company's balance sheets. These files will contain lists of all the assets and liabilities the company owns. This should go without saying, but the more reliable and complete a company's balance sheet is, the stronger and more trustworthy its stock price will be. If a company is loaded with assets, this could reflect the company's potential to earn more, thus increasing the stock value over time.

Another critical piece of data stock investors are always looking at and will be essential in stock choosing practices is the dividends a business pays out. 'Dividend' refers to the percentage or share of a company's profit that is paid out to shareholders. Dividends are used by companies to retain their shareholders who will invest money but will instead pay out a sum regularly.

If dividends are being paid out frequently, consistently, and of decent amounts, this is a clear sign that a company is profitable and doing well. Therefore, there's a good chance the company is growing, and investing in stock could be a worthwhile investment.

Using the Data to Make Decisions

It can take time to look through this data for each potential stock you want to buy, and for a good reason. If everyone had time to look through and choose stocks properly, then everyone would be doing it. It takes a particular set of skills, patience, and discipline to be able to go through, find patterns, and find profitable stock opportunities.

There are plenty of places you can find this information. Qualitative data can be found online, in newspapers and magazines, through online debates and expert opinions. If you have a mentor who's showing you the ropes, or friends who are also investing, they'll be able to show you information they've discovered, or highlight sources of legitimate information.

It's vital to consider where you're getting your information from because if the information is not trustworthy, then it's only going to trip you up.

How to Avoid Illegitimate Sources of Stock Information

If you read online that Apple stocks were going to rise by 200% tomorrow, you'd want to invest everything you had into that stock to make as much money as possible. With this in mind, you deposit a large sum of money, buy a load of stocks, and wait. And wait. And wait. The stock never rises. The article was fake. You've been duped.

This is what happens when you base your stock purchasing decisions on illegitimate data. However, in the age of constant content and fake news, how can you be sure the data you're using is coming from a trusted source? Let's go over a few tips.

Look for Legitimate Sources

First, look for where the information came from. If you're reading an article with no links whatsoever and points to no original sources of information, you should sign it off and move on straight away. There's no room in your mind for this kind of data that has no backup claims.

Any legitimate website will always link to authoritative sources of information that are trusted. Think the FT, other leading newspapers, and raw company data. When you go onto a website and click a link, you may notice it just bounces you around the website to other similar articles or posts made by the same writer. This means the claims are unsupported, and there's a high chance they aren't facts.

In short, avoid these 'sources' of information at all costs.

Consider Context and 'Cherry Picking'

It's effortless for writers to pick out stocks that make other stocks look good or bad. For example, I could say Stock A is up 60% over the last ten years. Wow, that sounds so good. However, when Stock B has gone up 80% and Stock C 100%, 40% doesn't look so good. It's easy to portray a 4% loss as being incredibly lucky or truly devastating, so keep an eye open and make sure you're aware of context when reading any information.

How Legit is Your Writer?

No matter what source of content you're looking at, make sure you're looking at the writer to see whether they are a legitimate, well-known writer, or just a random person on the internet. There are a ton of financial blogs out there that don't have the writers detailed, but it's merely an anonymous blog post. Avoid at all costs.

Likewise, some writers are made up and have a stock image photo as their profile picture, have no links to any social media profiles, and have no real connection to the financial world. Again, avoid them at all costs. If you don't know whether the writer is real, then you can't be sure the information they're giving you is.

Look at the Writer's History

If an investment writer only writes about their successes and never their failures, then you can bet they're probably not legitimate. Of course, there's the whole ego debate of why someone wouldn't want to tell other investors about their failings, but it's what honest stock investors and content creators do.

They show you both the good and bad sides of investing and will detail their experiences and share the lessons learned so you can learn from them, thus helping them build their audience. It's why they do what they do. Always refer to the track record of a writer and what content they've created. If a writer only has a list of massive success stories followed by a 'here's what you should do' section, they're probably trying to con you, or they've been incredibly lucky.

Avoid Penny Stock News

Penny stocks have been the notorious underbelly of the stock investment world, made famous in the mainstream society by movies like The Wolf of Wall Street. Many of the leading stock investors in the world will simply dismiss any website that ever considers writing and posting commentary on this industry.

Penny stocks are mainly just scams that will never pay off, and you're best off avoiding them altogether.

Scammers and con artists run the industry, and any website that advertises the industry in any other way is on the same level as this.

Dismiss Bot Content

It's a sad truth that we live in a world where robots and AI technology can write articles and create content that looks legit, but of course, it's not. All people who run websites need to do is feed their robot some financial facts, and the robots can create content that sounds semi-okay, but when you really look at it, instead of just skimming it, it's a load of rubbish.

Use Common Sense

Of course, listen to your gut when you're looking at information you want to use. Think about it. If you're reading an article and something doesn't seem right, something seems off, or the information doesn't add up, simply move on and go elsewhere.

Your common sense is there for a reason and will improve as you gain more experience within the stock investment world. You shouldn't ignore the fact you have doubts in your mind. Just take time to research whether a source is credible before continuing.

Just to recap everything we've just discussed, when looking for legitimate sources of information, you need to be looking at;

- Look for legitimate information sources

- Look for information context and cherry-picking

- Look at writer credibility

- Look for historical track records

- Avoid penny stocks

- Avoid bot-written content

- Use common sense

Bear all these points in mind when it comes to picking stocks based on the information you research. There are many websites out there that don't care about your investment but would rather make money through clicks and ads. Avoid them at all costs if you want to keep your portfolio healthy.

Chapter 8 - The Complete Stock Picking Checklist

We've covered a lot of information in the last few chapters, so we're going to dedicate this one to summarising everything into a handy checklist that you can refer back to at any time. Here we go;

- Choose stocks you're passionate about and interest in. If you don't care about the stocks you're buying, you're not going to have fun researching them or spending so much time dealing with them. Stock investment becomes a lot more fun when you get excited about what you're dealing with.

- Understand the company. Research and take the time to understand how the company you're investing in works. How does it make money? Is it innovative? Is there much competition in the industry? How does the company spend its money? What reputation does that company have with the public? The more you know about the company, the better.

- Work to your budget. Does the stock you're investing in work to your budget, or will you only be able to buy a handful because they're so expensive? Work to what you're able to work to, not just a popular stock that you think is good because it's expensive.

- Research the markets. Is it a good time to buying that stock in today's market? What's the reputation of the market and the company? Are people moving towards or away from this niche?

- How profitable is the stock? How long will it take to make money? Does the history of the company show that it's going to make money? Has the company got anything going on that could put it at risk of losing everything?

- What are the real-world conditions? Is public opinion for or against the company you're buying into? Are their international or global affairs that could affect sales within your preferred company? Is the company going through changes that could alter the financial condition of the company?

- Does the company data reflect the store? While a stock may be valued at a specific price, does the company's financial data reflect this? Are all the earnings and balances up to date? Are the ratios of the company reflective of the true state of the business?

- Is this stock diverse enough for your portfolio? All investors must have a somewhat varied portfolio to minimise losses and protect against risk. If you have one stock and it sinks, you'll be left with nothing. This is why diversity is essential.

- Is the information you're using trustworthy? Are you using legitimate sources of information to make your decisions, or are you taking someone's word because it's the news you've been waiting to hear? Are you using authoritative news sources, or just reading the first post that appears at the top of Google?

- Check in with your emotions. How are you feeling right now? Are you feeling grounded, centered, and focused? Have you just been subject to a significant loss or massive win, and you're riding on those emotions right now? Do you have hindsight bias? It's okay not to do anything and take a break if you need to realign yourself and your mindset.

- How does this stock compare to other stocks? When looking at all the stocks you're considering buying, how does this compare? Is this stock up there as a top contender, or are there better opportunities at your table that you should be focusing on?

- Carry out the last check. Think about what could go wrong. If this stock sinks, is it going to ruin you? How much money can you possibly lose from this investment? What time frame are you going to be working to? What price are you planning to sell? Is this a worthwhile investment?

You need to be asking yourself these questions to make sure a stock is worth buying. These aren't the only questions you need to ask, and there are a ton of variables you need to think about, but as a beginner stock investor, these points are a great place to start.

Check them off every time you think about buying a stock to ensure you're making the most informed decision possible. Right, onwards with building your portfolio.

Chapter 9 - Setting an Investment Budget

We've spoken a lot about setting and sticking to an investment budget. It would be easy to simply take every cent you earn and chuck it into your brokerage account, but you'll have no money to live on, and you'll have no way of tracking how much you're making. It's also far too risky because if you lose everything, you'll quickly find yourself in a financial crisis.

You need to be money smart.

At the centre of everything you do, you have your investment budget. This is how much money you're willing to risk investing, and you need to ensure won't go over this figure. Remember, we've already spoken about being disciplined and sticking to your investment plans. Even if you're investing and making a ton of money, you mustn't go over budget with your investments. This is the beginning of going down a very slippery slope into financial insecurity.

In short, setting an investment budget is an essential part of the process. Here's how to do it.

How to Set an Investment Budget

First, figure out how much you're spending on expenses to live day by day. There are two types of expenses to consider; non-discretionary expenses and discretionary. Non-discretionary, as the title suggests, is the type of expense you can't live without. Sure, you can make changes in terms of how much they're going to cost you, but these are required payments you have in your life.

Non-discretionary expenses are payments like rent, electricity bills, your phone contract, grocery shopping, and any transportation costs you need to pay, such as train tickets or all the expenses that come with owning a car.

The easiest thing to do is to open your bank statement and go through it, writing down all your non-discretionary expenses and how much they cost. Simply add all these numbers together, and you'll have your non-discretionary expenses total.

Let's say you earn $2,000 per month, and you spend $1,000 on non-discretionary expenses, you'll have $1,000 left to invest. Although, you may want to consider your discretionary expenses first.

These include things like;

- Leisure activities

- Outings to concerts or sporting events

- Gifts for Christmas or birthdays

- Going out for a meal

- Buying a luxury item

- Any impulse purchases

- Media subscriptions (like Netflix)

- Holidays and vacations

- Gym memberships

Unless you're incredibly strict with your money, then chances are you have a few of these expenses in your monthly statement. Nobody is expecting you to cut out everything and go entirely towards investing. You need to be able to live your life and be happy. However, if you want to take investing seriously, you may want to do away with some of the more frivolous purchases that you don't actually want or need.

Cut out the spending you're not really interested in and add up the expenses you do want to keep. Going back to our example, if you spend $500 on discretionary purchases per month, you then have $500 a month left to invest. This is more than enough to get started.

But hold on. Remember, you need to be careful and prepared with your money. If you haven't created an emergency fund, you may want to put $250 away into savings and then invest the over $250. You don't want to spend everything and have nothing if your car breaks down, or some other necessary purchase arises.

So, make sure you don't forget to keep an eye open and plan for hidden fees and unexpected events; you can set a comfortable budget for you. In our example, we settle for $250. With this budget, you must make sure you stick to it.

Of course, that's not to say you can't update your budget in a year when you evaluate how things are going, but you must be strict with yourself in sticking to what you set. If you start developing a bit of a winning streak and making lots of money, you may be tempted to chuck $1,000 into your investment account.

If the investment doesn't pay off straight away, that's not to say it won't pay off in a few months, but it may leave you struggling in the short-term, meaning you may end up needing to take your investment out to pay bills and then you'll have lost all your progress. It's essential to make sure you stick to your budget, and that it's a budget you can afford.

Chapter 10 - Choosing Your Long-Term Investment Strategies

We've spoken a lot about not investing for short-term gains, but rather aiming for long-term sustainable growth on your portfolio. Sure, investing $1,000 and turning it into $10,000 in a jumping stock is the dream, and everyone would get involved if investing was that easy, but the real world doesn't work like that.

What's more common is buying a stock for $500 and watching drop to $250 and then cursing yourself because you made such a wrong purchase, but then within nine months, it's worth $1,000, which is when you sell it and profit. That's how proper, long-term, active investing works.

So, you're probably wondering how you create such a strategy?

There are plenty out there, and it depends on who you're speaking too. You could talk to two highly experienced investors who have spent decades in the industry, and they'll detail two very different strategies, but they'll both work in their own way. You'll also develop your own way of working in time, designing your own strategy as you go.

But that's not very helpful right now, which is why we'll dive into four of the most common strategies out there, detailing how they work and the pros and cons of each.

Strategy #1 – Growth Investment

Perhaps the most common investment strategy, growth investing is all about looking for strong stocks with a very low risk of falling back down. A good way of putting this is that growth investors are looking for the sliced bread of stocks. The next greatest and best thing that's going to come out and they're going to stick with it.

However, if a tech company declares they're going to send a rocket into space and build a base on the moon in the next six months, sure this sounds like the next best thing, but using common sense, you know this simply isn't possible. Growth investment is not about being irresponsible with your investments; it's about being smart and looking for those niche opportunities.

Another example of this would be to look at whether solar and green energy has a future in the world before investing in a solar panel company. Is national security going to be tightened before investing in a weapons company? Is Instagram still going to be around in two or three years before investing in Facebook? These are the sorts of questions you need to be asking yourself.

Is the industry of the stock looking for a solution that the stock is offering? If so, and you think it's a stock that's going to grow over time, then you've got yourself a growth investment stock. Most growth stock investors will not take chances on random potential opportunities but will instead look at the evidence to almost guarantee that their investment is going to pay off in the long term.

If you find a stock you can see growing; you'll want to look at the history of it to know whether it's something you should be considered, or whether the risk is too considerable. If you see steady and consistent growth over the last decade, then the chances are this is a safe bet. Look for consistent and sustainable growth and earnings from the company before buying.

There are cons to this strategy to think about. Firstly, since the company is growing, you can bet that more capital will be going into growth than there are dividends so that the payouts can be small compared with higher-risk stocks. Fewer payouts mean less cash in your pocket, but this is the price you pay for the relative security of steady and reliable growth.

Is this the strategy for you?

Well, there is research that shows that value investment (see below) is better and more profitable over the long-term than growth investment, but that doesn't mean that growth investing is not successful. If you're looking for small but steady long-term profits, then you want to be looking at growth investing.

If you're looking to pick growth stocks, it's important to note there aren't any real figures or metrics you can use, apart from looking at the individual company growth history. Just remember, growth stocks are usually the first to get hit when poor economic conditions hit, and if you're borrowing money to invest, you're not going to see much return whatsoever.

Strategy #2 – Value Investment

Value investors are the sorts of investors who shop for bargains on the market and try to turn a profit with them. Think The Wolf of Wall Street styled investment with their penny stocks, although that's not going to be happening here.

What you're looking out for is affordable, inexpensive stocks that have huge potential but are currently undervalued. This means you need to know your industry well, understanding what works and doesn't work, and then being able to pick stocks you think are going to have a huge potential.

For example, if you're into tech stocks, you may see a company with an app some onto the exchange. They have a few decent apps under them, and they're doing okay, but nothing special. You read an article in a magazine about a new app they're developing, and you think it's going to make it big.

You buy their stocks right now since they're so affordable, and when the app is released, and the stock's value rises dramatically, you've made a boatload of money in the process. It's a great way to earn money, but it is slightly risky because the stocks might not pay off, as well as the potential to shrink in value.

There are obvious pros to using this strategy. Your initial investments don't need to be expensive, and there's the chance to receive a massive payoff if everything goes well. The problem is that this strategy could literally take years to pay off. So many value investors invest a ton of money and don't wait the long game because they're too impatient and they miss out.

When you look over the last decade of stock trading from 2014, the average payout on big stocks is around 6.7%, whereas value stocks only give out a 5.5% return. Why is this? Because people are too quick to cut and run from their strategies. Remember, if you're playing the long game and sticking to your guns, you're going to get the most significant returns!

When value investing, you don't need to pour through thousands of stocks trying to find one that might be a good deal. There are a ton of mutual funds out there that showcase potentially undervalued stocks that can be a great reference point to get you started. If you look at a resource like the Russell 1000 Value Index, this is a fantastic place to find undervalued stocks, but remember that anybody can see this index, so the opportunities aren't rare.

If you want to find some nice stocks that are undervalued, another great place to start is to look at the price-earnings ratio, also known as the 'P/E.' You can do this by filtering results on your brokerage website. If you can find a low P/E ratio, which is calculated by taking a stock price and dividing it by its earnings-per-share figure (EPS), this means you could be paying less than $1 for current earnings.

Of course, you can't wholly base your value stock findings on this figure alone, but it's a really good place to start. There is the risk that these low ratio numbers are caused by inflated accounting numbers, which can happen temporarily, which is why you need to be smart about making a decision around it, as you should be with all investment decisions you make.

Strategy #3 – Dollar-Cost Investment

Also known as DCA, dollar-cost investment is all about investing over and over again over time, but while this is what you're doing with the other strategies above, there is something a little different. It's more of a cocktail of strategies that you can flux with however you like.

For example, let's say you pay $1,000 into your brokerage account every month to invest with. You use a Robo-advisor account, so there's no extra thinking, you just put the money into your account and let computers and algorithms do the work. There's no risk from the human side of things because you're as disciplined as possible and just letting technology do its job.

The problem with the other strategies we've mentioned here is that human error is always present. Even the most experienced investors will feel the urge to invest when prices are low, only to buy and then have to bear the prices dropping even further. It can be disheartening and emotional for even the most seasoned investor. This is especially the case if you're borrowing investment money from an external source and investing it all at once.

Instead of this, dollar-cost investing means putting a disciplined amount of money into your account every month and letting the system do its thing. Because you're adding a little bit of money here and there, the average per-share cost is much lower on purchases, thus making you money long-term.

When deciding on this strategy, you need to be thinking of three main points of consideration.

Firstly, you need to think of the total figure you're investing in. Then, couple this with the frequency of purchases you're making, plus for what duration of time you're going to be investing. When you consider all these points, you'll be fully in control of your budget and your spending, you can manage your purchases effortlessly, and you'll be protecting your investment.

This is perhaps the most common form of investment strategy, especially for beginner investors because it reduces how much risk you're potentially subject too. However, if you're looking to invest a large amount of money in one lump sum, this may not be the strategy for you. If you're starting out, putting a bit of money in, letting it do its thing, putting a bit more money in, and so on, is an easy way to enter the investment world.

Strategy #4 – Momentum Investment

Imagine riding a surfboard along a gigantic wave in some tropical part of the world. It's blissful and exciting, and there's no other feeling on Earth that can compare to it. That's what momentum investing is. It's about cruising from win to win to win for as long as possible before bailing on the wave and crashing into the ocean, hopefully in one piece.

Momentum investment is one of the most complicated strategies and one of the riskiest, so if you're starting out, you may want to try a safer approach until you get your bearings. Still, it's essential to know what this strategy is so you can incorporate it for yourself. Remember, the decision is all yours.

Momentum investors take a ton of data and use it to fuel their decisions. They accumulate as much knowledge as possible before making a final call. They use computer software and experience to discover and highlight patterns in the market on stock prices before making a purchase.

So, to summarise, it's all about buying undervalued stocks that are rising rapidly, then selling those stocks as close to the peak as possible before investing in another rapidly growing stock and riding that wave as close to the peak as possible and then repeating the cycle.

Simple enough, right?

Well, not quite. Rob Arnott of the Research Affiliates company researched whether this type of investment actually paid off. It turns out that at no point in investment history has a U.S fund with 'momentum' in the name actually outperformed the benchmark figures. That includes both fees and expenses.

While the idea is very profitable, there's a problem that comes in the form of trading costs. This is referring to the fees and commissions taken by brokerage firms.

When you buy and sell a stock, you pay a trading cost fee, or your brokerage receives a commission. As a momentum investor, you could be selling trade after trade every week. Maybe even multiple trades a day, and this can become incredibly expensive long-term and ultimately leaving you with not a lot of profit.

With this in mind, if you do want to keep riding that wave, you need to be on it with your trading every hour of the day. You need to be using every app (okay, not every app, but at least one app) to wake you up in the night to tell you when a stock has reached a certain level, and it's time to sell. You need to be on the ball every hour of every day. This is how small the profit margins and risks are.

However, if you like to have a break every now and then, which is highly recommended because you can't physically be on it all day every day, some ETFs are designed to help momentum styled investors keep up the pace. These ETFs will basically give you access to an assortment of stocks that match your momentum criteria that you can work around efficiently without having to do too much research.

A Mention of Short Selling

Within aggressive momentum traders, there's a process known as 'short-selling' which is used to boost returns on what could otherwise be small profits. It works by letting momentum investors return a small profit when a stock price drops. It sounds strange, but here's an example.

Say a short seller investor borrows 100 shares at the price of $200. They had an idea that those stocks were going to drop in value but bought them anyway. The seller then sells those shares immediately at the price of $200 and waits for those stocks' prices to drop. The company then repurchases the 100 shares at $50.

This means that the short seller has spent $200 on the original sale, then made it back for $200, whereas the company has only gained $50 from the purchase, meaning the short seller has made $150 from the transition.

This may sound incredibly profitable, but it's also one of the riskiest forms of trading stocks. If you invest $200, you can lose $200 at the snap of your fingers. Let's say you've borrowed the 100 shares, but the price doesn't drop, and they go up instead. Now they're worth $500. You now owe the company $500, meaning you've lost that much altogether. The capacity to lose in this many is practically limitless.

All in all, unless you know what you're doing, have heavily researched, or have a mentor working with you and showing you the ropes, it's probably best to avoid this kind of investing, but it's definitely something you can think about in the long-term.

Do you see a strategy you like the look? Of course, you may feel the need to speak to an investment advisor or do more research to see what investment strategies are out there, so you can choose what is right for your individual situation. Check how you're going to be investing, what type of investors you want to be, how often and how much you're going to be depositing into your account, and what your investment goals are.

With all this in mind, you should be able to create a strategy that works for you.

Chapter 11 - How to Benefit from Investing in a Crisis

As much as the world relies on the economy, it is in no way stable, and crises occur all the time. There was a global financial crisis in 2008 because credit was being handed out to anybody and wasn't being paid back. This ultimately caused global stock markets to crash, which send many investors (and governments) into panic mode and wiped many other investors out.

Even in 2020, there has been a market crisis, thanks to the COVID-19 pandemic. The S&P 500 Index fell by over 37% in early February in just five weeks. At the same time, stock markets in the G7 fell by 20%. This is not the first time this has happened, and it's almost guaranteed that it won't be the last. That's how edgy trading stocks can be.

However, that doesn't mean that money can't be made during a financial crisis. In some cases, just surviving the crisis with minimal losses could be what you're aiming for, and that's fine. Many investors don't even make it that far. You just need to know what you're doing and be proactive in making smart decisions.

How to Take Advantage of a Financial Crisis

Of course, the most obvious way to make the most of a financial crisis is to take advantage of the low value of stocks. As stock prices and values plummet left, right, and center, this means there's never been a better time to buy. All those juicy, high-value stocks you've had your eye on for some time but never had enough investment to commit too?

Well, now they've fallen right into your price range, if not becoming more affordable than that. Don't' mistake it; there's still a risk involved in buying these stocks. If the company is unable to bounce back from a crisis, you'll be operating at a loss, so you still need to pick wisely and follow the market to educate yourself before making a decision.

Making this kind of move requires a ton of mental discipline to carry out. You need to be patient and calm. One panic move made out of fear, and you could mess everything up completely. Just look at the past to help you retain this optimistic mindset.

When a crisis has occurred in the past, it usually takes a while, but the majority of stocks will get back to roughly where they were, if not better. There are a few exceptions to the rule in both directions, of course, but most stocks are sold out of fear, which is what affects the market.

One study carried out by the Ned Davis Research Group discovered that over 28 global crisis's that had occurred throughout the world, covering everything from 9/11 terrorist attacks and World War II battles, the stock markets always overreacted and sold stocks out of fear, only for them to return to their original values a short time after. That's 100% of the time.

Think about the event in which Japan attacked Pearl Harbour. The S&P500 Index fell 4% and then continued to fall by 14% over just a few months. Investors were in hysterics. However, by the end of the wat, more than 25% was added to the Index year on year, on average.

The lesson to be learned here; markets always overreact. Do your own thing.

For those investors who ignored the fear and panic and bought shares at low prices and sold them again while high, these crises were very profitable experiences. However, this isn't the only way to benefit from a crisis.

Think back to the housing crisis of 2008. Since people weren't able to pay back their mortgage repayments, many houses were repossessed and sold off cheap to cover the credit costs. Who bought the houses? Investors did, of course. Investors purchased the homes at cheap rates and then held onto them for a few years before selling them again once the housing market had bounced back, thus making their money back and profit on their original investment.

The same happened with 'vulture' investors, who went around buying up companies that were struggling to pay back their debts. If a company wasn't surviving the crisis, but the business and assets' fundamental data looked solid, investors would buy them up, wait for a crisis to blow over, and then do them up to make them profitable again.

While these are key investment strategies to consider, you're going to need a lot of investment in the first place to take part. While houses and businesses were cheap value-wise, they're still not inexpensive. As a beginner, you may not be able to partake in such strategies, which is why below you'll find some more affordable options on how you can keep yourself afloat.

Focus on Low-Risk Investments

Perhaps the best move, or at least the safest move, you can make is looking into low-risk investments that can almost guarantee a payout, even if it is minimal. As above, sometimes taking advantage of a crisis means just being able to get through to the other side, so play it safe.

Look for companies that have decent cash flow and not a lot of debt. If you're confronted with a high-risk opportunity, it's probably best to avoid it.

Look for Consumer Staple Investments

Some products just don't get affected by recessions. These are usually luxury items that may differ slightly, but most people will continue to buy them. This category includes things like groceries and food, alcohol, and tobacco. Beverage and food companies are usually a safe bet. Be careful not to go for anything too luxurious though.

Look for Recession-Proof Opportunities

Hand in hand with the consideration above, some opportunities will continue to pay off during a recession and can sometimes even grow. Brands like budget stores can pay off well in a crisis situation, such as grocery stores, funeral services, and cosmetic companies. All of these are worth checking out since they always have a year-long demand, and the supply is relatively constant at all times.

Diversify Your Portfolio

If you're only buying stocks from one industry, or one specific niche, you're dramatically increasing your chances of losing when a crisis hits. We've already spoken a lot about diversifying your portfolio, which is most important in times of need. Even when it comes to low-risk, consumer staple stocks we talked about above, ensure you have diversity.

In the recent COVID-19 pandemic, previously reliable staples like tobacco actually dropped for the first time because COVID is a medical virus, and an increasing number of people became health conscious because of it. Try to broaden your horizons as much as possible.

Consider Dividend Stocks

Stocks are a great way to create passive income for yourself and your portfolio, and they work very simply. You pay a company for some dividend shares; they keep your money but pay you a sum of the company's profits. If you want to be really safe, you could look for companies that have increased their dividend payouts for two decades or more, just to ensure you're most likely going to receive a payout.

Consider Precious Metal Investments

The final approach you could take to surviving and maybe even profiting from a crisis would be to think about investing in precious metals. The most commonly traded precious metal is, of course, gold, because it has consistently retained its value in times of crisis throughout the past, even up until this day. Silver tends to work well, as well.

As you can see, there are a lot of options and directions you can consider if you find yourself investing in a time of crisis. Again, this is vital for you to remember, do not let your emotions get in the way. Waking up in the morning and seeing a ton of red percentages on your television screen is scary, but you can overcome it.

Keep your head on straight, and your mind focused. Don't let emotions like fear and anxiety dictate your decisions and ruin what you've worked so hard to create.

Chapter 12 - What is an EFT, and Why Is It Important?

Throughout this book, we've spoken a lot about EFTs. They've cropped up here and there, and if you don't know what they are already and how they can benefit you as a stock investor, this is the chapter for you.

An EFT stands for 'exchange-traded funds' and works similarly to mutual investment funds, except with a difference. The stocks found in an ETF are traded in a similar way to stocks, and still hold assets and bonds, but do so at a much lower operating cost than traditional bonds. There are a ton of benefits that come with this, so let's look at each point in detail.

What is an ETF, and How Does It Work?

An ETF can be a little bit complicated to understand if you're new to it, so take your time, there's no rush. ETF work like stocks, except there are multiple stocks in a collection, known commonly as a basket of securities.

Here's an example.

The S&P 500 ETF (trading code SPY) tracks the extremely popular and highly coveted S&P 500 Index. Within the ETF, there are multiple investment types available, including the stocks, bonds, and more. However, all of these investment types are traded under one name, and therefore only one price.

Since the confusion and complexity of trading everything separately have been removed, there's more transparency on tax, easier and more creative ways to trade, and can create increased transparency within the market.

While ETFs are traded just like stocks on the market, there is a slight difference that an ETF can vary in price throughout the day as stocks are bought and sold.

Traditional mutual funds are only officially sold once the market has closed, and the prices are then updated. ETFs are incredibly popular, a level of popularity which is only increasing. In 2018 alone, over $4 trillion was invested into exchange-traded funds.

Since ETFs contain a variety of investment opportunities under one name, these are excellent choices for beginner investors who are looking to diversify their investment portfolio. There are plenty of ETFs out there that have hundreds, if not thousands, of stocks within them across all industries, and those that specialise within specific niches.

What's more, within the ETF industry, you'll find various types of ETFs. These include;

Bond EFTs	Include bonds like government bonds, state and local bonds, and corporate bonds.
Commodity ETFs	ETFs that look into substance commodities, like crude oil and precious metals.
Currency ETFs	ETFs that invest in foreign currencies around the world

Industry ETFs	ETFs that look at securities within various segmented industries, such as gas and oil, tech, banking, and the sorts.

The Benefits of Buying ETFs

You already know that ETFs are great ideas if you're looking to add some diversity to your portfolio. There are some other great benefits like tax transparency and low operating costs, but what else do ETFs really have to offer?

Firstly, ETFs are incredibly flexible. Since they can be traded and have their price change at any time, you could be trading the same ETF multiple times per day if the markets change that much. This gives you way more control over your investments and how long you want to hold onto them.

This level of flexibility also continues down into what makes the ETF itself. Any underlying asset within the ETF, whether that's bonds, stocks, and commodities, can be traded in real-time throughout the day on an hour to hour basis if you want to, although it's not recommended that you do.

Secondly, you get to spread your risk through diversification. The current state of the market means there are practically endless ETFs to choose from, ranging from ETFs based in different countries, different currencies, styles, makeups, industries, and every sector you can imagine.

Every kind of asset class, commodity, and currency can also be found within modern-day ETFs, which grants you so many more opportunities with how you want to fulfil your personal investment strategy. This means that even if you have a portfolio made up of mainly tech companies, you could invest in a currency ETF that will give you access to trading some of the world's most profitable currencies.

Cheaper, More Affordable Costs

All operating costs on the markets are managed by managed funds, no matter how the managing fund is set up. Within these costs, you'll find fees and expenses like admin costs, custody costs, portfolio management fees, marketing expenses, and more. As an investor, you must look into your expenses to ensure you're not spending too much on fees that are ultimately jeopardising your final return on capital.

Since ETFs contain all securities in one place, the operational costs of managing this fund drop considerably. For example, your typical open-end fund company is required to send out statements and reports to their shareholders regularly. That simply has to happen, but not with ETFs.

Since the companies only need to share the information with authorized bodies who are owners and personally create the EFT units, this process becomes a lot more streamlined and cost-effective, generating savings that are then passed onto you.

Once created, the ETFs then go on sale just like any old regular stock on the exchange, so you can simply buy and sell them for the discounted prices.

The Tax Benefits of ETFs

The final benefit you'll need to consider is that ETFs have two very important tax benefits compared with traditional mutual funds. Due to the way mutual funds are structured, they endure higher capital gains tax than ETFs, and ETFs only need to pay capital gains tax when the investor makes the ETF sale.

Mutual funds work differently this way since they have to pay capital gains taxes on the investment for the complete duration of the stock they have, rather than just paying tax once the investment is being sold. This can save you such a huge amount of money in the long term and is well worth considering.

However, it's not all good news. If you're looking at dividends offered by EFTs, this is a very different story. There are two types of dividends; qualified and unqualified. Unqualified dividends mean, of course, that you won't get paid a dividend fee.

If you want your ETF to become qualified for dividend payouts, you need to hold the investment for 60 days before the dividend payout date, and you'll need to pay tax on the dividend, which will vary between 5 and 15%, depending on your income tax rate.

How to Buy and Sell ETFs

Buying and selling EFTs is as simple as buying and selling stocks. You just need to head over your brokerage account website and make a purchase of one that you like the look of, checking them over in the same way you would a traditional stock (refer to the chapters above).

There are also lots of dedicated ETF brokers out there on the internet you can look at, as well as Robo-advisor alternatives if you don't want to spend too much time worrying about the logistics of your investment.

Chapter 13 - Moving Forward with Your Portfolio (Final Thoughts)

And there we have it.

We've reached the end of our journey, and you should now have an extremely comprehensive understanding of how to enter the stock market as a beginner investor and have all the tools and techniques you need to make a decent start.

Remember, as you gain experience, you'll be able to grow your portfolio exponentially. The more experience you have, and the more understanding you have on your specific niches and industries, the more advantage you'll have in the markets, and the more likely you are to make the best, most profitable decisions.

There's no need to rush. The trick to investing is being patient and keeping your emotions out of your decision-making process. As soon as emotion enters the game, it's over because you're never going to be deciding a grounded state of mind. The investment game is not one that makes overnight successes, but instead grows winners over decades.

Keep your eye on the ball. Keep your mind focused and disciplined. Stick to your rules and guidelines. Educate yourself as much as possible. Never stop learning. Good luck with your investment journey.

Disclaimer

This book contains opinions and ideas of the author and is meant to teach the reader informative and helpful knowledge while due care should be taken by the user in the application of the information provided. The instructions and strategies are possibly not right for every reader and there is no guarantee that they work for everyone. Using this book and implementing the information/recipes therein contained is explicitly your own responsibility and risk. This work with all its contents, does not guarantee correctness, completion, quality or correctness of the provided information. Misinformation or misprints cannot be completely eliminated.

Design: Natalia Design

Printed in Great Britain
by Amazon